LIL **DIAMONDS**
BASEBALL GEMS IN THE MAKING!

Reggie Hammonds

Library of Congress Cataloging-in-Publication Data is available.

ISBN# 978-0-578-74077-5

Lil Diamonds
Jersey City, NJ 07304

LIL DIAMONDS is a registered trademark.

Originally published as Lil Diamonds in the United States of America in 2014 by the author.

Books are available at special discounts when purchased in bulk for teams, premiums, and sales promotions as well as for fundraising or educational use. Special editions or book excerpts can be created to specification. For details, contact the Special Sales team at the address below or send an email to info@lildiamonds.com.

LIL DIAMONDS

ACKNOWLEDGEMENTS

Mom and Dad, thank you for your endless love, dedication, strength, and devotion to our family. Your tireless support in all of our endeavors was paramount in our success on the baseball field and in life. We are heavenly blessed to have you as our parents.

To my younger brothers thank you.

Kenny, for always being a voice of reason with humor, strength, and unwavering character.

Jeff for carrying the torch to higher levels with honor and class. You are a great example of a scholar athlete and a true professional baseball player.

Veronica and Randy – thank you for your love and inspiration.
I love you.

My baseball coaches throughout the years, thank you for your commitment, dedication, and insightful instruction. Through innovative drills and creative practice sessions, baseball was engaging, fun and highly competitive.

Thanks to:
- Dad: Coach, mentor, role model
- Jim Sochan: Coach, Scotch Plains/Fanwood High school
- Jasper Furham: Coach, Scotch Plains/Fanwood
- Ron Wellman: Coach, Northwestern University
- Bill Bryck: Scout, Pittsburgh Pirates organization
- Mike Quade: Coach, Pittsburgh Pirates organization
- Ed Ott: Coach, Pittsburgh Pirates organization

LIL DIAMONDS

FOREWARD

Our family has baseball in its DNA and we have for generations. My grandfather played baseball. My father played and coached baseball. He passed his passion for the sport on to his sons, starting with me. My earliest memories of baseball are playing with my dad on the front lawn when I was about five. He would consistently and intentionally:

- Play catch with me
- Work on my swing
- Hit grounders and pop fly balls to me
- Show me how to round the bases

REGGIE HAMMONDS
Nashua   OF

He did the same with my two younger brothers. He taught us focus, discipline and a winning mindset. The result?

Kenny played and excelled in Varsity baseball and football in high school.

I was the Captain of three sports in high school – baseball, basketball and football. I led the State of NJ in hitting with a .595

batting average. I received full scholarships for football and baseball to Northwestern University and was drafted for baseball twice.

Jeffrey received a full baseball scholarship to Stanford University, where he was a two-time All American, represented the U.S. Olympic Baseball team, was the 4th pick in the 1st round of Major League Baseball Draft and went on to make the 2000 MLB National League All-Star Team!

Between the two of us we were drafted four times. I was drafted by the Seattle Mariners and Pittsburgh Pirates. Jeff was drafted by the Toronto Blue Jays and Baltimore Orioles. I went on to play Minor League Baseball for three seasons before a career-ending injury forced me to stop. Jeff went on to play Major League Baseball for five teams in 13 seasons.

This level of success in one household is a testament to my Dad's commitment and dedication to give his three sons the baseball know-how and competitive edge to compete and succeed on the baseball diamond.

I will attempt to do for you what my Dad did for us.

After leaving baseball, I became a certified high school history teacher. I then went on to build a career on Wall Street.

I decided to take what I learned from my father as a youngster to create the Lil Diamonds program. Why "Lil Diamonds"? Because this book is written specifically for you to help teach and instruct little kids on the fundamentals of baseball. I have used two key tools to develop this program. First, my insights derived from playing baseball at all levels. Second, I used my experience as a teacher to hone my skills in lesson planning and mastered the art of giving information to kids in a way they would understand and

LIL DIAMONDS

retain. I'm giving you a gift to give your child – a road map for success in the game of youth baseball.

The Lil Diamonds™ program is designed to make your child successful in playing the game of baseball while also having lots of fun. Keep in mind that when your child is successful the game *becomes* fun. At an early age **Fun Is a Factor.** The more fun your child has playing baseball the more time he/she will spend working on their baseball skill set.

The goal of this program is to simplify and assist you in helping your child build a firm foundation through:

1. Understanding the game of baseball
2. Developing their skill set
3. Benefiting from successful performance and
4. Having loads of fun

LIL DIAMONDS GUIDE

About Lil Diamonds Youth Baseball Program

LIL DIAMONDS

INTRODUCTION TO LIL DIAMONDS

SUCCESS=FUN+CONFIDENCE

Lil Diamonds is a program whose mission is to teach and instruct the fundamental foundation of playing baseball.

This program gives you the hands-on instructions to effectively steer your child towards baseball success with a series of clear concise teaching techniques and drills. The Lil Diamonds program is designed to assist your child in developing his/her baseball skills each and every week. Eventually, the weeks turn into months and the months turn into years. There will be major accomplishments and minor setbacks along the way. Throughout the book, I've offered ways to minimize and overcome setbacks. This feat is achieved from viewing selected visual illustrations, coaching instructions, and participating in selective baseball drills designed to

LIL DIAMONDS

enhance your child's overall skillset. The best part is that you can achieve a level of good success with just the use of simple, inexpensive equipment and your endearing love.

Every good effort has motivation behind it. Let me tell you a small story that has always reminded me of the value of the Lil Diamonds program. Back in the early 90's, I met a neighbor, a mother who had an 8-year-old son. The mother enrolled the young boy in the local Little League, and they were excited. One Saturday morning, I saw them in the lobby before going to a game and the young boy was overjoyed to be in his uniform and he could not wait to begin playing the great game of baseball. A couple of weeks later, I noticed the little boy and his mother going to his game. However, he did not have the same glean in his eye and looked as if he didn't want to go. A week later, I saw the two of them again. I asked how baseball was going and the boy looked down and said "ok". His mother shook her head and whispered, "he had a few bad games". I told the young boy to hang in there and that he would do better the next time. Well, unfortunately things did not get better, and he later decided to stop playing.

As I look back, here was a young boy who could have benefitted from some personal coaching. A few simple baseball drills and words of loving encouragement probably would have made all the difference in the world for this young kid. The biggest contributing factor to his waning interest in baseball was a lack of success. It eliminated the prospect of having fun. Here was a young boy who could have and should have benefitted from someone with good baseball experience and specific, illustrated instructions. Well, here is my chance to do so.

This Lil Diamond program is designed to make sure young children who need an edge in gaining and maintaining the necessary skill set to play baseball can do so.

Regardless of the circumstances, being a dedicated single parent or a grandparent, this program is for you. If you are parents with limited time to dedicate to your child's baseball aspirations, this program is for you. Even if you are a parent or relative who has the time but just wants to give your child a special edge so they can experience good success on the baseball field, this program is for you.

WELCOME TO THE LIL DIAMONDS PROGRAM!

Let's take your child's ambitions of playing baseball and shoot for the stars and shine bright. To aim high and expect the very best. Through systematic drills and repetition, let's help him/her experience a good level of success on the baseball diamond. Remember, you can't have fun without success, and you can't have confidence without success. **Success is the key.**

Every diamond began as a lump of coal which, through pressure and a chain of events, created the world's most precious stone. Let's take your child and through drills, practice, repetition, encouragement and love, create a Lil Diamond.

In time, your child will shine bright and go from being a diamond in the rough to earning the distinction of becoming a Lil Diamond!

Have fun and good success!

Let's begin...

LIL DIAMONDS

Chapter 1

Rules of
Engagement

Understanding the game of baseball begins with grasping the "Field of Play". The baseball field is aptly referred to as the **baseball diamond**. The actual baseball diamond is displayed above.

On the Field of Play these are the following features:

- Home Plate
- Bases
- Pitcher's Mound
- Foul Lines
- Infield
- Outfield

LIL DIAMONDS

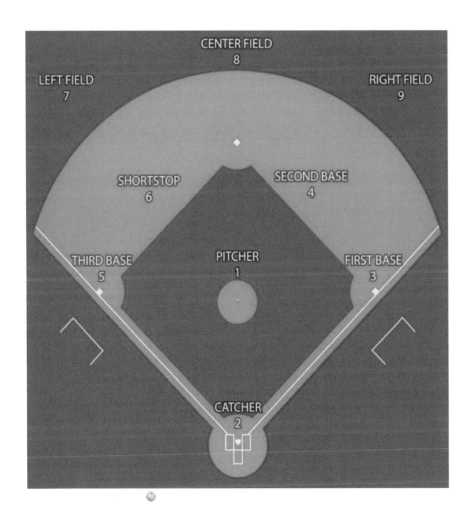

Let's discuss the key elements on the Field of Play.

LIL DIAMONDS

HOME PLATE

This main base initiates the action and records the runs. It determines the strikes and balls called by an umpire. All hitters' start at home base and their goal is to get on base either by getting a hit or by receiving a walk (4 balls). Runs are recorded when hitters round all the bases (1st, 2nd and 3rd third bases) and ultimately, reach home base again.

BASES

First base (1B) |Second base (2B) |Third base (3B) |Home plate

Again, the object is to round all the bases ending with Home Base/Plate, without making an out. Once this feat is achieved, the offensive team scores a run. At the end of the game the team that has the most runs wins the game.

LIL DIAMONDS

PITCHER'S MOUND

This is the area on the baseball diamond where the Pitcher stands and throws the pitches to the batter. Distances between the mound and home plate vary with age and levels of play. The white slab in the middle of the mound is called the pitching rubber. The purpose of the rubber is for the pitcher to push off of it and throw to home plate. This is an activity that comes with age (8+ years old).

FOUL LINES

These white lines extend from home plate on opposite sides of the playing field pass the infield into the outfield, all the way to the outfield wall. The foul lines assist the umpire in determining if a ball is fair (in play) or foul (out of play).

LIL DIAMONDS

Chapter 2

Position Players

Let's explain the defensive unit. The defense consists of nine (9) players. Each position has its own unique qualities and requires a specific set of skills. Let's breakdown the dynamics of the different positions. The nine positions are organized with six (6) players in the infield and three (3) players in the outfield. This makes up the complete defensive unit of a baseball team.

LIL DIAMONDS

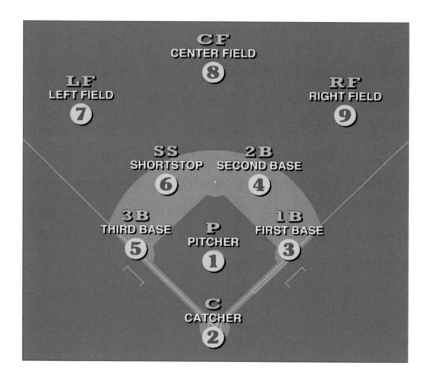

INFIELD

Infielders are players in the diamond area of a baseball field. These position players must be good ground ball fielders because most of the balls hit to infielders are ground balls. The majority of the hit balls to infielders are ground balls. Infielders also need to always be alert and quick to catch hard line drives off the bats of hitters. Occasionally, there are high pop flies but very few at this early age (5-8). Because of the lack of power by the hitters most of the hit balls stay in the infield area.

Let's breakdown each position with a brief summary.

First let's talk about the battery that runs the team – the pitcher and catcher. Why is it called the battery? Because, it starts and puts the game in motion.

LIL DIAMONDS

PITCHER

The pitcher is a key player who usually has a direct effect on the outcome of a game. A pitcher needs to have a strong, accurate arm and have leadership qualities. He is the focal point of the defensive team. He is the player who throws the ball to the catcher which puts the game in motion. The pitcher's goal is to get the batter out either by:

- Strikeout (3 strikes)
- Groundball out
- Pop up/fly ball out

When playing T-ball (age 5-7) the pitcher does not participate and is not part of the defense. The pitcher position becomes more relevant at 8+ years old.

LIL DIAMONDS

CATCHER

The catcher's position becomes important when the pitcher is involved at 8+ years old. The catcher is a demanding, tough position and requires involvement in every play. The catcher calls and catches the pitches, fields, throws out and tags runners. That sounds like a lot and it is. Here's a good thing, it is a position that not everyone wants to play. Once you are good at this position people will take quick notice and high praises will follow. Your catching talents will be in demand.

At the youth level, there is very little interaction between the pitcher and the catcher because pitched balls are not always required. Therefore, I suggest playing other positions and if you decide you really want to be a catcher, you can always try out for it later.

1ˢᵀ BASEMAN

Playing 1ˢᵗ base is a very fun and active position. The 1ˢᵗ baseman is involved in a lot of plays. The 1ˢᵗ baseman must be a good catcher and fielder. He/she is the receiver of throws from other infielders, many of which are not accurate at this level of play. The 1ˢᵗ baseman is key and must learn to catch throws from other infielders while keeping one foot on first base. As the level of play increases the role of the 1ˢᵗ baseman will continue to heighten and become more valuable. (e.g. pick off throws from the pitcher and catcher and relay throws from the outfield).

2ⁿᵈ BASEMAN

Second base is another fun and active position. You need to be quick and nimble with good fielding and catching skills. You do not need a strong arm but you must be accurate throwing to 1ˢᵗ base. Later in higher levels of play one will learn to:

- Turn double plays
- Tag out runners who are trying to steal 2ⁿᵈ base
- Receive cut off throws from the outfield

This all comes in later years. Keep in mind, at a young age many of the hit balls by right-handed batters will go to the right side of the infield (2ⁿᵈ base and 1ˢᵗ base). Therefore, this is a busy position and a preferred position for young ball players.

SHORTSTOP

The shortstop is the best defensive player on the team. A true natural leader. This player needs to be a good fielder with a strong accurate arm. At this age, this is asking a lot. Just fielding the ball and throwing to 1ˢᵗ base is challenging due to manning the largest area in the infield. In addition, the shortstop will eventually need to receive and tag out runners, turn double plays and receive relay throws from the outfield. In time and with lots of practice, the

LIL DIAMONDS

shortstop will either get better or move to a less challenging position.

Keep in mind, the room for error is larger for shortstops because of this challenging, demanding position. Therefore, your best athlete on the team is a good candidate for the short stop position. In time, a true shortstop evolves, and the position becomes second nature.

3rd BASEMAN

The 3rd baseman needs quick reflexes, great fielding and catching skills and a strong accurate arm for the throw to 1st base. In youth baseball, the right-handed batters are not inclined to pull the ball down the 3rd base line. So, the 3rd baseman does not see a lot of action until more advanced levels. Occasionally, a good hitter at even this young age will hit the ball hard down to third base. Therefore, it's a good thing to have a good fielder with quick reflexes play third base.

THE OUTFIELD

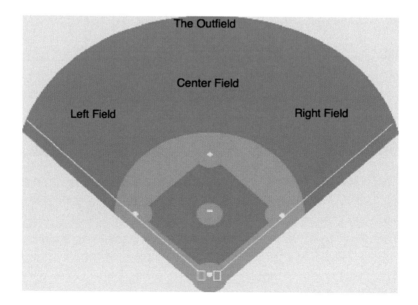

The Outfield

Center Field

Left Field   Right Field

LIL DIAMONDS

The outfield positions require the skills of catching fly balls (either stationary or running) and fielding ground balls. At the youth level outfielders are on the lip or the edge of the infield. Keep in mind, at this level of play many balls are fielded just beyond the infield and there is a need to quickly field and throw the ball back to the appropriate base with accuracy.

Seldom are there fly balls that carry to the outfield positions. Most are groundballs and few line drives that get through the infield. Once the ball is hit to an outfielder in youth ball, they should either:

- Throw to the to the base which is ahead of the runner in order to prevent the runner from advancing further or;
- Quickly run the ball back to the infield.

Now let's go over and emphasize each of the outfielder's traits and strengths.

LEFT FIELDER

The left fielder needs to be a good fielder with an accurate arm. They also need to back up the most active infield position, which is shortstop. Backing up means to run to the area behind a play in order to retrieve the ball in case of a missed ball or throw.

CENTER FIELDER

The center fielder has the largest territory to cover, thus speed and leadership abilities are needed. He/she actively communicates to the other outfield positions (Left Field and Right Field). Also, the center fielder needs to constantly back up the shortstop and second base positions. In older leagues, throws from the catcher on stolen base attempts also needs to be backed up.

LIL DIAMONDS

RIGHT FIELDER

The right fielder needs to have a strong throwing arm because they must make the long throw to third base. The right fielder also needs to backup throws to the 1st baseman from other infielders.

Let's Recap:

Between 5-7 years old, your child will play defense in the infield or on the edge of the infield/outfield. Why? Because there are very few hit balls that will travel further than the infield.

LIL DIAMONDS

Chapter 3

Choosing A Position

Now for the sake of not actually choosing your child's position but to inform, usually the shortstop, catcher, and centerfielder positions are the more challenging defensive positions. Why? Because they are leadership positions and are very active. Each of these positions are very skilled and at times verbal. They need to communicate with other players.

Let me explain further:

- The catcher is in constant contact with the coaches as well as calling signals (hand signals directing the pitcher what pitches to throw) for the pitchers. (9+ years old).

LIL DIAMONDS

- The shortstop is the captain of the infield. He/she communicates with the coaches, infielders and helps in the positioning of other infielders and outfielders. He/she is the most skilled infielder and will receive more hit balls, most of the catcher's throws on stolen base attempts and will be the relay for most of the outfielders' throws. He/she is a very important position player and should be viewed as the point guard of the defense.
- The centerfielder has the largest real estate or range to cover of any position player. Highly skilled fielder and in older leagues will instruct the other outfielders where to position themselves.

The other position players round out the 9 position players of a baseball team defense. Each position is important in its own right, however not as crucial to a team's defensive success as the catcher, shortstop and centerfielder. Therefore, if a position is too challenging, there is nothing wrong with changing to a less challenging position. Normally, a coach will recognize this and make the necessary changes for the benefit of the player and team. In time, young players can develop and grow into challenging position players.

Catching and Throwing: The cornerstones of every defensive player. Let's talk about catching first.

CATCHING

Teaching your child the correct catching technique is paramount. This one ability could make the difference between a child wanting to play the game of baseball or being too afraid of getting hit with the ball that he/she doesn't want to play for fear of getting hurt.

First and foremost, initially use a soft ball. A tennis ball is highly recommended. Baseball is a game of repetition. Practice, practice, practice. The more your child does a specific exercise the better

LIL DIAMONDS

he/she will be, and this is definitely the case when it comes to catching a ball. Keep in mind, I have found that at the ages of 5-7 results may not happen all at once. This is a skill that is not mastered until a much later age (9+ years). So be patient and encourage, encourage, encourage. Now let's begin.

Remember to use a soft ball (tennis ball, nerf ball, squishy ball, etc.).

Key Points to teach your child:

- Keep your eye on the ball
- Have both hands ready, with arms relaxed and extended toward the incoming ball

Bend the elbows to absorb the force of the ball

- Catch the ball away from your face. Either to the right or the left of your head

- Watch the ball into the glove and squeeze it
- Soft hands should be the mindset. Imagine the glove is a pillow and you are receiving the ball gently. Absorb the impact. Do not stab at the ball.

DRILL 1: WALL BALL

Once again, the best way to learn how to play catch is with a soft ball like a tennis ball, a nerf ball, a squishy ball and then progress to a t-ball. (Which is softer than a baseball and should be used until the age of 9).

Remember, this is not a rush skill. Catching a baseball cleanly evolves over time. I've found that one of the best ways to nurture the skill of catching is to use the "Wall Ball Drill", which is a favorite

LIL DIAMONDS

drill of mine. Find a wall such as a hand ball court, the back of a school, your apartment building or the back of your house and let your kid play catch with the wall. This drill can be done with or without a glove.

Let your kid practice throwing and playing catch by him/herself. No instructions needed. Just a freelance exercise of your kid being him/herself and developing a natural rhythm of playing catch.

Every session should be at least 15 minutes and after a few sessions, your child will extend the time on his/her own. Why? Because it's a freelance drill with little involvement from you. It's a drill that children will enjoy doing all by themselves. The sheer fun of throwing and catching the ball will propel your child to engage in this fun activity. All you must do is marvel and give words of encouragement along the way.

After a few sessions, if they have not used a glove, begin to have your child use a glove. Begin extending the time to least 20 minutes and give encouragement but do not critique. (At least not yet) This a "Fun Factor" drill. Hugs and high fives should be given to your child during and after the drill. Encourage, encourage, encourage. Now if your child can log in 14 sessions at 30 minutes, the total time will be 420 minutes-7 hours of repetitive throwing and catching. You will clearly notice that your child has improved dramatically from the initial session. Real results!!

You can always video the 1st few sessions and compare it to the 14th session. Whoa! What a difference a day makes. The key is to make this drill fun at all times, all he/she needs is a supporter/cheerleader. Be that supporter/cheerleader!! Allow your child to freelance, and let their natural instincts take over and good results will happen. Let it happen!

DRILL 2: PLAY CATCH

The next stage needed for your child to become a future Lil Diamond will require your active participation. If you are not physically able, not a problem. Find a trusted family member, friend or a teammate/ classmate of your child who is able to play catch. Preferably, in the case of a teammate/classmate, this should be someone who is of same age or slightly older.

At first, play catch without a glove. Start the catching exercise 5 to 7 feet away for a few sessions until he/she is catching the ball consistently. Be patient because the eye-hand coordination may take a while. Then slowly extend the distance by 2 feet, to 7-9 feet, then another 2 feet to 9-11 feet.

The key is to master the short-range catch! This is a MUST!! Keep in mind that making this catching exercise fun is the key!! Make sure

LIL DIAMONDS

that you (or the designated catching partner) and your child play catch in a playful no pressure atmosphere.

This catching exercise infused with encouragement and fun will produce real results only if you child enjoys the interaction. Once again, make sure that you use a soft texture ball. After a few sessions of playing catch with you or another person, your child's confidence will gradually grow. Keep in mind this is a repetition drill. The more your child plays catch the better he/she will become. The key is to have fun while doing this exercise, which will make your child a willing participant. If it's fun, they will enjoy it enough to do it again and again. In time, your kid will ask you to play catch with them. How about that? Expect it!

DRILL 3: GROUND BALLS

Fielding ground balls is as equally important as catching fly balls. At any position, the majority of the hit balls will be on the ground, especially at this level. Use a soft textured ball and proceed to roll the ball on the ground from 10 feet away. Make sure your child bends their knees and shuffles their feet in a manner that is quick and fluid. After your kid has a good grasp of fielding the ball cleanly, then proceed to gently bouncing the ball.

Keep the distances short (less than 10 ft.). If they are having a tough time fielding the balls shorten the distance from 10ft to 7ft. Remember the key at this stage is building confidence. In time, once your child has a good command of fielding the ground balls cleanly (without missing or bobbling), then extend the distance.

Another good exercise is to catch 5 balls in a row without dropping or mishandling a tossed or rolled ball. This is a good drill from the standpoint of setting a short attainable goal and accomplishing the goal. Once, your Lil Diamond accomplishes this neat feat, celebrate with high fives!

A Lil Gem

If at first your kid is just not into it, I've found that using a ball that lights up upon impact adds instant fun to catching drills. You can find such a ball at various toy stores. Keep in mind, lighted balls are made of rubber, which tends to be harder than a t-ball. Therefore, play catch at shorter distances of less than 7ft for thrown balls and less than 10ft for ground balls. The lighted ball will engage and excite your Lil Diamond at this early age. Remember the more fun the better!

LIL DIAMONDS

Chapter 5

Throwing

Throwing the ball at this age is not as important as catching at this level. (5-8 years) Why? Because before one can throw, one must make the catch. Throwing is a skill that will grow in importance as time goes on. By playing "Wall Ball" and simply playing catch with a counterpart your child will naturally work on the mechanics of throwing.

First, let's talk about how to grip a ball. The proper way is to put your thumb under the ball with two or three fingers on top. Throwing with the pointer and index fingers across the seams is

LIL DIAMONDS

the best way to grip the ball for accuracy and speed. Don't worry about the seams at this age.

Below are key points on throwing properly:

- Eyes on the target
- Legs apart and foot on throwing arm side behind the body
- Arm back and in an upward position
- Front shoulder turned towards the target
- Step towards the target with foot opposite throwing arm.
- Right hander steps forward with left foot.
- Left hander steps forward with right foot
- Push off on the back foot as the throw begins and end with weight on the forward foot
- Release the ball

DELIVERY

Be sure to stress picking up the lead foot and stride towards the target. Once the lead foot hits the ground, the torso and hip should rotate toward the intended target. Release the ball over the head and in the front of the body and follow through. Remember to focus on the target until you release the ball.

LIL DIAMONDS

FOLLOW THROUGH

The follow through is more important at an older age when speed and accurate throws can make the difference of winning and losing games. At the t-ball age, simply focus on the delivery, throwing the ball overhand and aiming at the target.

DRILL 4: THROWING

When doing the "Wall Ball" drill (mentioned in the catching section), a good exercise is to mark an "X" on the wall with chalk and instruct your child to throw and hit the target.

Make sure the distance is no more than 10 feet for the first few sessions. Instruct your child to throw at the "X" on the wall 10 times and keep record of the successful hits on the marked "X" on the wall. This will get him/her into the habit of throwing to specific object. When throwing in games begins to matter, your child would have already developed an aptitude for accuracy. Also, by playing catch, your child will begin to focus on hitting a target (e.g. glove). Make sure you give your Lil Diamond a good glove target and when he hits your glove let your kid know by saying "good job"!

A Lil Gem

Keep in mind: Accuracy is more important than velocity. Also, I want to stress how important it is to throw over the top and not side arm. Why? First, throwing side armed lessens the accuracy of the throw. Second, throwing side armed puts more strain on the elbow and the shoulder area and could lead to significant arm problems. Therefore, throwing over the top is the way to go! This proper motion will protect the arm, increase velocity, enhance accuracy and reduce the chance of injury.

LIL DIAMONDS

Chapter 6

Hitting

LIL DIAMONDS

Now, for the most important part of baseball -- hitting. This is the difference maker. If your child is a good hitter, he/she could be average in every other aspect of the game (fielding, throwing and running) and still be a star. This is where the action is. This is where headlines are made, accolades are given, scholarships are secured and, in some cases, draft picks are selected. Now let's enter the world of hitting:

- Grip
- Stance
- Stride
- Swing
- Finish

These are the mechanics of hitting. Let's start with the batter's box and then we'll focus on each of the above points and then I will talk about the importance of one's individual style.

THE BATTER'S BOX

The batter's box is the designated hitter zone that is situated on both sides of home plate. As a batter, you're required to stay within the white lines of the batter's box.

GRIP

Grip the bat firmly (don't squeeze). Put your hands together above the knob with the middle knuckles lined up. Hold the bat with both hands until contact is made, then drop the bat and run to 1st base.

STANCE

Young players should be comfortable in the batter's box. A coach should not try to make every batter assume the same stance. Each child is unique and as such their stance should be different. The key is to have a comfortable stance. Given this important point, let's talk about the basics of a good stance.

- Feet should be apart the same distance as the shoulders
- Toes pointed towards the tee/plate
- Knees slightly bent with weight centered on the balls of their feet

- Upper body bent slightly at the waist
- Eyes focused on the tee or pitcher
- Bat at a 45-degree angle to the hands and not straight up but slightly tilted
- Elbows out from the body and flexed pointing towards the ground

STRIDE

The stride is the triggering mechanism to begin the motion of the shoulders, hips and knees as the pitcher releases the ball. A small

LIL DIAMONDS

stride of the front foot towards the pitcher's mound to initiate weight distribution begins the swing sequence.

SWING

The legs and the hips initiate the swing. Remember to keep your eyes on the ball, shoulders level, bat and head steady. The actual swing should be level to slightly upward in order to bring the bat through the center of the ball. It's easier said than done and takes practice. Remember to keep your head down, extend your arms and follow through. Focus on making contact and do not swing too hard.

As your child, engages in taking swings (or as they say in baseball terms "cuts"), he/she will eventually form their own natural style

LIL DIAMONDS

and find their own comfortable stance. The more comfortable a hitter is at the plate the better.

This takes time and many years of taking swings or as they say, "cuts" to achieve a natural, comfortable swing. Many baseball players will even change their swings completely. However, good hitters will settle down into a swing that is natural and comfortable.

FOLLOW THROUGH

Swing as if you were hitting three balls back to back to back. This will allow for an extended swing and proper follow through. A nice,

balanced position is desired when the swing is over. Quickly, drop the bat and run hard to first base. Remember to always hustle out of the batter box.

A Lil Gem
Now always remember, the game of baseball is a game of repetition and the more your child swings and makes contact with ball, the more confident they will become. Therefore, make it fun. Allow for the drills to be repetitive enough that your child has success. Then the confidence level will increase. Remember, Fun + Success = Confidence, especially when it comes to the art of hitting. Confidence is our ultimate goal. Once you have confidence then great things happen.

Let's stay on hitting a little longer and recap:

- Feet spread shoulder width apart
- Bent knees
- Body in a slight crouch
- Weight on the balls of feet
- Grip bat, hands together above the knob
- Hold bat firmly. Don't squeeze.
- Bring bat up and away from the body
- Keep shoulders level, bat and head steady
- Eyes on the ball
- Short step with the front foot at the start of the swing
- Swing level and bring the bat through the center of the ball
- Watch the bat hit the ball and keep head down
- Weight shifts to front foot, back foot stays planted on the ground
- Extend arms and follow through with your swing
- See where the ball is hit
- Drop bat and run hard to first base

These are the hitting fundamentals. The goal is to incorporate the above steps into a smooth, fluid, consistent swing. To accomplish this feat takes time and plenty of practice. If your child can log in 50 swings in a given week that's a good start. It sounds like a lot, but 5 sets of 10 swings with intervals of rest in between the sets is a good start.

If this is too much for your kid (every kid is different) then do 3 sets of 10. This amounts to at least 200 swings a month. (50 swings x 4 sessions =200) During the six months from March to August, this amounts to a least 1,200 swings a season for your youngster. The 1,200 swings do not include his/her swings during the team's practices and games.

The 50 swings a week are Lil Diamond program swings. By utilizing hitting drills (tee, soft toss, and pitched-to swings) in a constructive, methodical way and encouraging your child's swings helps build the proper hitting foundation.

LIL DIAMONDS

DRILL 5: T-BALL

The first piece of hitting equipment you should buy is a hitting tee. A tee is basically, a rubber plate with a rubber pole. This is designed for mastering your child's hitting mechanics. Let's bring the "Fun Factor" back into the equation. Whew! Just in time. This singular piece of equipment is essential for any baseball hitter. In the case of 5-7 year olds, the tee is pivotal and essential for your child's success and overall confidence. The key is to make it fun.

A ball is placed on top of the rubber pole at the center of the plate. Your child can now work on his basic mechanics without having to hit a moving ball. The ball is stationary and in full view. Your child is now in control of timing and distance and, when he/she is ready to swing, they can with confidence. The object is to hit the ball off the tee squarely. Thus, the term "t-ball". At this young age a t-ball league is perfect. By hitting the ball off the tee, your child can work on their mechanics and have a high degree of success as well. This is so important at an early age.

The tee work or should I say "tee play" is a great drill and worthy of application. Getting through the hitting zone and making solid contact with the ball is the goal of any hitter. Having your child position themselves at the plate properly, striding and transferring their weight while keeping their head down, with their eyes fixed on the ball, engaging the swing, and watching the bat hit the ball. Priceless…

Let's recap t-ball:

- Child can work on their mechanics at their own pace
- Eyes are fixed on the ball at the point of contact
- Builds confidence through repetitively hitting the ball
- Your involvement and interaction with your child during this passive but very important drill is great.
- Major Leaguers still use this timeless piece of equipment to correct THEIR mechanics

DRILL 6: SOFT TOSS

The next hitting drill is an exercise called soft toss. Position yourself on the side of your child, on an angle that is almost parallel/even to your child's swing. Be safe! Be sure that you are not in the way of your child's swing and if your child lets go of the bat, you can get out of the way.

Now, softly toss the ball to your child, aiming at his/her belt buckle and, when the ball enters the hitting zone, your child should swing. Make sure the swing is level with a slight uppercut. You can do this drill near a chain linked fence or any other enclosure, in order to easily collect the balls. Make sure that you and your child are at least 10 feet away to make sure that the ball doesn't ricochet back at either of you. This drill is a great way to establish timing in your child's swing.

The hand-eye coordination in picking up the ball as it leaves your hand, striding, swinging and making contact is another great way to enhance hitting skills and build confidence. This particular drill is a nice bridge between hitting off the tee and live pitching.

Let's do a recap of the soft toss drill:

- Your child is making contact with a moving object
- The distance is shorter than a normal pitcher, thus the success rate of hitting the ball is better
- Your child's confidence level is growing. Now he/she is hitting a moving object!
- You are interacting and encouraging your child and the bond between you and your child is growing beautifully.

This is another drill/exercise that beginner players can use that major leaguers use. How about that!

LIL DIAMONDS

DRILL 7: FREE SWING DRILL

In this drill, you are the pitcher. Once again, use a soft textured ball and stand approximately 10 feet away. This is another drill to instill confidence in your child while increasing their skill level. In today's competitive world, you will encounter young players being pushed hard by their parents, coaches, peers etc. to hit live pitching even if it's underhanded. I've even seen t-ball leagues begin with the tee and then it's completely taken away by the third game and the young kid is pushed to hit live underhand and sometimes overhand pitching.

A Lil Gem

Try not to critique misses. This is another "Fun Factor Drill." After about 5 sets (rounds) of 4 pitched balls totaling 20 pitches and swings, stop and hug your kid and tell them "great job". It does not matter if he/she hits most of the pitched balls, a few, or none at all. This is a starting point, something to build upon.

Keep in mind that your child is going to love your positive reinforcement and overall interaction of playing baseball with someone who is patient and loves them. This particular drill should be one of total encouragement and full of accolades. Why? Because the Free Swing drill is more complex than the previous drills. It requires the total package of hitting a baseball. Picking up the ball from the pitcher's hand and engaging all of the components of a baseball swing. The highlight is making contact with the ball. Your child will sense he/she is gradually getting better and the overall feeling of experiencing small accomplishments is going to be truly exciting and beneficial to their baseball development.

As you do this drill, you will see an improvement in your child's overall approach to hitting. They will begin to plant his/her feet and hands properly and get through the hitting zone. Be patient. The key is the repetitive nature of this drill.

LIL DIAMONDS

There will be days when your child will regress. Just know that this is a temporary setback and keep encouraging your child. If they miss and the swing is a good-looking swing, make sure you say "good swing! Just keep your eye on the ball". If you make a bad pitch and he/she misses the ball, make sure you say "bad pitch! Let's get ready for the next one!" At this impressionable age, maximize the positives and minimize the negatives. Always end the session by telling your child how well they are doing and to keep up the good work. If they had a bad day tell him/her they will do better next time and give them a hug and a high five. The only reason why I incorporated the free swing drill is because, this particular drill will give your child an edge if during a t-ball game or practice the tee is removed and the coach decides to pitch to the team.

Believe me, as I previously mentioned this scenario happens in many so-call t-ball leagues and at least your child will have had experience hitting live pitching. So it's better to be prepared for this (removal of the Tee) happening and be ready by performing this hitting drill.

The LD program is designed to keep you one step ahead. Have loads of fun participating, encouraging and bonding with your child during this drill!

To my dismay, I've watched young players swing and miss live pitching 10-15 times before they make contact. Or even worse, after missing so many pitches the coach grabs the tee and sets it up so the child can swing off the tee. This is never a fast set-up and it's embarrassing for the child and their parents.

I believe t-ball should be just that – t-ball and nothing else. However, if you find yourself in a league where your child is being pushed to hit live pitching even if it's underhand, it is better to be prepared than not be. So, let's begin...

LIL DIAMONDS

As I mentioned, use a soft textured ball and have your child stand approximately 15-20 feet away. You can do this drill in the park, on a handball court, in the backyard or on a baseball field. Preferably, in a place with no car or pedestrian traffic and no parked cars. Go ahead and unscrew the rubber tube off the tee and use just the plate. This drill requires that you have at least 4 balls. Tell your child to get into his/her stance and take a few practice swings. Now softly throw the ball underhand and have your child take a few rips at the pitches.

Let's recap the hitting drills:

- T-ball
- Soft Toss
- Free Swing

All three drills are routinely performed by major leaguers, but yet simple enough to be done by children. These drills will always be part of your child's baseball career. However, these drills are the cornerstones of your child's hitting foundation. Having your child feel comfortable with these drills will greatly benefit your lil diamond's hitting skill set. Just do the drills and, in time, watch the steady improvement. Exciting!!

Hitting is a skill that your child needs to acquire in order to do well in baseball. Pursue and capture the art of hitting through these fun drills and remember repetition of the drills is key during your child's early ages.

If success is not sudden, that's baseball. If success is fleeting that's baseball. If your child is successful 3 out of 10 times he/she is considered a good hitter at any level. If your child is successful 4 out 10, he/she is a great hitter. Anything above that is considered a phenom.

LIL DIAMONDS

Lil Gem

Remember, hitting is vital when it comes to your child's overall success. Keep in mind, at the end of the game, the one thing a child will remember is how many hits they had and how hard they hit the ball. If your child can hit, he/she will play. It's that simple. He/she will want to play because they are experiencing success and thus having fun! Loads of fun!

LIL DIAMONDS

Chapter 7

Base Running

Tell your child, when he/she runs to first base, to run on the balls of their feet. Make sure they look at the base their running towards. This will help them run in a straight line. When running to first base, run slightly outside the foul line. Tell your child to run through 1st base and not to jump on the base. Why? This could cause injury.

LIL DIAMONDS

Once on first base, watch the next hitter and anticipate him/her hitting the ball. Once the ball is hit, hustle to second base.

The same applies to running to 3rd base and running to home base. Make sure you listen to your coach's instructions.

DRILL 8: RUNNING DRILL

Have your player stand at home base in a batting stance and then say "Go!". Your player then swings, drops the bat and runs to 1st base as fast as they can. Once at 1st base, instruct your Lil Diamond to keep one foot on first and the other foot positioned and pointed towards 2nd base. Then say "Go!" and yell "hustle!". It is important to always hustle and exert maximum effort – all the time, especially

LIL DIAMONDS

when running the bases. Then have your Lil Diamond run to second base as fast as they can. The same applies to running from 2nd base to 3rd base and then 3rd base to home plate.

Give your kid a big high five when they cross home plate! This is a drill that you can practice with your kid on any baseball field or open space. This is a good drill to perform as the last drill of the day. It's an enthusiastic way to leave the baseball field on a great note! Everyone running, laughing and giving high fives.

**Final Thoughts...
Developing the
Mind of a
Champion**

I have found that the best time to perform the drills is a day or two before a game. This puts your child in what is a called the "zone". What is the zone? The zone is getting familiar with the skills necessary to perform well and this comfortable state of mind is then transferred to when the lights are on (game time). Where did I learn this?

I remember my Dad taking me out in the backyard and pitched peas to me and I'd have to hit the peas with my bat. He would do it until I was hitting the peas consistently. Once I got the point where he knew I was locked in and focused on the task at hand, he'd stop, smile and say "good job". The next day, I'd go to the game and the baseball would look like a basketball!

My Dad's drills helped all of us succeed in baseball. In hindsight, our Dad, through systematic, consistent drills made sure his sons gained an edge in playing baseball from a young age.

LIL DIAMONDS

Let the Lil Diamonds program do the same thing for your little one. Use the visuals, instructions and drills in this program and your child will experience success.

Be sure to visit www.LilDiamonds.com to get more resources to help your Lil Diamond.

Start now! Your child will shine bright while playing the great game of baseball and earn the distinction of being a Lil Diamond!

Have Fun and Good Success.

LIL **DIAMONDS**
BASEBALL GEMS IN THE MAKING!

Fun Facts & Conversation Starters

1. Baseball fans eat enough hot dogs to stretch from Dodger Stadium in Los Angeles, California to Wrigley Field in Chicago, Illinois. During MLB games, about 25,500,000 hotdogs and 5,508,900 sausages are sold every year.

2. During World War II, which brought prosperity to most blacks as well as whites, Negro baseball became a $2 million-a-year business, probably the most lucrative black-dominated enterprise in the United States at that time.

3. Each baseball is hand sawn and can only last six pitches before it is retired. This means 5-6 dozen of baseballs are used in each game.

4. Brooklyn Dodger president Branch Rickey, a one-time big-league catcher and manager, had put into motion a secret plan to find and sign an African American player. It culminated on October 23, 1945, when Jackie Robinson, a first-year shortstop for the black Kansas City Monarchs, officially signed a contract with the Dodgers. He spent the 1946 season with the minor league Montreal Royals. In 1947 Robinson was promoted to the Dodgers, becoming the first black player in the major leagues in 63 years.

5. The shortest player to ever bat in a major league baseball game was Eddie Gaedel (1925–1961), who was 3 feet, 7 inches tall. He came to the plate for the St. Louis Browns against the Detroit Tigers on August 19, 1951, during part of publicity stunt[8]. Today Edward's autograph sells for more than Babe Ruth's.

6. The longest baseball game in history lasted 26 innings. On 1st May, 1920, a game between Brooklyn Dodgers and Boston Braves lasted for 3 hours and 50 minutes which is almost equivalent to three whole games. It consisted of 26 innings.

7. No woman has ever played in a major league baseball game. American sports executive Effa Louise Manley (1897–1981) is

the first and only woman inducted into the Baseball Hall of Fame.[8]

8. The first known reference to the word "baseball" was in a 1744 publication by children's publisher John Newberry called A Little Pretty Pocket Book.[11]

9. Roberto Clemente is the first Latin American and Caribbean player to win a World Series as a starting position player (1960); to receive a National League MVP award (1966) and a World Series MVP award (1971).

10. In 2008, Dr. David A. Peters found that sliding headfirst into a base is faster than a feet-first slide.[6]

11. The initial baseball game between two black teams was held in 1859, in the state of New York. The two teams were the Henson Base Ball Club of Jamaica of Queens and the Unknowns of Brooklyn.

12. Baseball gloves have evolved more than any other piece of the sport's equipment.[6]

13. The Cleveland Indians signed Larry Doby, a fleet, hard-hitting infielder from the black Newark Eagles, making him the first African American in the American League.

14. The New York Yankees were the first baseball team to wear numbers on their backs, in the 1920s. They initially wore numbers based on the batting order. Babe Ruth always hit third, so he was number 3.[4]

15. The Yankees' Mickey Mantle holds the record for the longest home run on record for a 565-foot clout hit at Washington DC's old Griffith Stadium on April 17, 1953. As a switch hitter, he was batting right-handed against left-handed pitcher Chuck Stobbs from the Washington Senators.[8]

16. There is a rule in baseball that before every game, an umpire should remove the shine from the new baseballs by rubbing them with mud from a creek in Burlington County, New Jersey.[4]

17. Chicago Cubs outfielder Rick Monday became a national hero when he rescued an American flag from two men who were trying to set it on fire in the outfield at Dodger Stadium during

LIL DIAMONDS

a game on April 25, 1976. The 25,167 fans gave him a standing ovation and burst out singing "God Bless America."[8]

18. The first U.S. president to throw the ceremonial first ball was William Howard Taft (a former semipro baseball player) on April 14, 1910. American presidents, except Jimmy Carter, have been throwing out the first ball on Opening Day ever since.[8]

19. "The Star-Spangled Banner" was performed for the first time at a sporting event on September 5, 1918, in the middle of the 7th inning of Game 1 of the World Series between the Boston Red Sox and the Chicago Cubs at (rented out) Comiskey Park.[8]

20. Ken Griffey Sr. and Ken Griffey Jr. became the first father and son to play in the major leagues as teammates for the Seattle Mariners in 1990. On September 14, 1990, they hit back-to-back home runs, creating another father-son baseball first.[8]

21. Minor league pitcher Jackie Mitchell (1913–1987) is famous for striking out both Babe Ruth and Lou Gehrig in succession in the 1930s. She was promptly banned from Major and Minor League Baseball.[8]

22. Famous baseball movies include *The Bad News Bears* (1976), *The Pride of the Yankees* (1942), *The Natural* (1984), *Bill Durham* (1988), *Bang the Drum Slowly* (1973), *Field of Dreams* (1989), *Moneyball* (2011), *42* (2013), *A League of Their Own* (1992), *Bingo Long Travelling All Stars & Motor Kings* (1976) and *Eight Men Out* (1988).[12]

23. Visiting teams wear (at least mostly) gray uniforms so fans can easily distinguish between the visiting team and the home team. The tradition dates back to the late 1800s when travelling teams did not have time to launder their uniforms and, consequently, wore gray to hide the dirt.[4]

24. The first pro baseball game ever to be aired on television was on August 26, 1939. It was a doubleheader between Brooklyn and Cincinnati.[8]

25. "Soaking" was a very early baseball rule that allowed a runner who was off base to be put out by throwing a ball at him.[4]

26. The team with the most players in the Hall of Fame is the San Francisco Giants, who have 24 Hall of Famers.[8]
27. From 1995 to 2001, every seat at Jacobs Field was sold out every night for 455 baseball games in a row. The Cleveland Indians retired the number 455 in honor of their fans.[8]
28. The last major league ballpark to install lights was Chicago's Wrigley Field in 1988. Until then, the Cubs did not have lights and played all their home games in the daytime.[8]
29. Boston Red Sox player Jimmy Piersall celebrated his 100th home run by running the bases backwards. He was an eccentric player who inspired the book and movie *Fear Strikes Out*, which chronicle his battle with bipolar disorder.[8]
30. In 1989, NBC's Gayle Gardner (1950–) became the first woman to regularly host Major League Baseball games for a television network.[8]
31. When baseball great Lou Gehrig retired from the game due to amyotrophic lateral sclerosis (ALS), he said in his farewell speech that he was "the luckiest man on the face of the earth." His speech has been called the "Gettysburg Address of Baseball.[8]
32. Toni Stone (1921–1996) became the first of three women to play in baseball's Negro League over its 40-year history. Baseball historians called her the "female Jackie Robinson." At one time, in 1953, she was the fourth best batter in the league.[13]
33. Dave Winfield, a member of the MLB Hall of Fame, was drafted by 4 professional teams in three different sports – MLB (San Diego Padres), NBA (Atlanta Hawks), ABA (Utah Jazz) and NFL (Minnesota Vikings).
34. While baseball games today last about 3 hours, the fastest game ever played in major league history lasted just 51 minutes on September 28, 1919. The New York Giants defeated the Philadelphia Phillies 6-1 at the Polo Grounds.[8]
35. The most innings ever played in a Major League Baseball game was 26 innings on May 1, 1920, when the Brooklyn Dodgers played the Boston Braves.[8]

36. The longest game on record was between the Chicago White Sox and the visiting Milwaukee Brewers on May 9, 1984. The game lasted 8 hours 6 minutes and went 25 innings.[8]

37. The record for the least amount of people at a baseball game was set in 2011 when the Florida Marlins played the Cincinnati Reds. Due to Hurricane Irene, just 347 people attended the game.[8]

38. Ricky Henderson holds Major League Baseball records for career stolen bases, runs, unintentional walks and leadoff homeruns.

39. A "gentleman's agreement" among the leaders of what was then called "Organized Baseball" (the major and minor leagues) erected a color bar against black players from the last years of the 19th century until 1946, although these leaders rarely admitted its existence.

40. The most valuable baseball card ever is the 1909 Honus Wagner T206 baseball card, worth about $2.8 million.[8]

41. In 1990, the Negro Leagues Baseball Museum opened in Kansas City, Missouri where the first league began.

42. On July 17, 2010, the U.S. Postal Service issued a se-tenant pair of 44-cent U.S. commemorative postage stamps, to honor the all-black professional baseball leagues that operated from 1920 to about 1960.

43. In 1919, the Chicago White Sox earned the name "Black Sox" when eight players were accused of intentionally losing the World Series. The eight players were banned from baseball for life, including "Shoeless" Joe Jackson, one of baseball's all-time greatest hitters. Because he was kicked out, he is also ineligible for the Hall of Fame.[8]

44. Baseball bats in the minor and major leagues are made from wood. However, metal bats are used at the college level.[6]

45. Even though two baseball bats weigh the same, they may feel lighter or heavier when they are swung. The "swing weight" differs according to the distribution of mass in a bat.[6]

LIL DIAMONDS

46. Researchers note that the most successful baseball hitters have brains that can process visual information faster than normal. They have the ability to detect the spin of a ball as soon as the pitcher releases it and claim they can see the ball in "slightly slower" motion.[6]

47. A big-league player can hit a 90-mph pitch with more than 8,000 pounds during the millisecond that the bat is in contact with the baseball. The ball leaves the bat at a speed of 110 mph.[6]

48. A player increases his chance of hitting a home run if he hits the baseball at the bat's "sweet spot." This spot is an area between 5 and 7 inches from the barrel end of the bat. When a player hits the sweet spot, there is less vibration, and the bat makes a satisfying "crack" sound.[6]

49. Since 1983, major league players have been required to wear helmets with at least one earflap to protect the side of the head facing the pitcher. The latest helmets also provide increased protection to the back of the head.[6]

50. Only one major league player has been killed by a pitched ball. Ray Chapman of the Cleveland Indians was fatally hit in the head on August 16, 1920, by a ball thrown by Yankee pitcher Carl Mays.[6]

51. During a swing, a baseball bat may travel about 80 mph at its peak.[6]

52. The Yankees retired Don Mattingly's number (#23) making him the only Yankee to have his number retired without having won a World Series with the team.

53. The first-ever radio broadcast of a major league baseball game occurred on August 5, 1921, by radio station KDKA in Pittsburgh. The first place Pirates beat the last place Philadelphia Phillies 8-5 at Forbes Field. It also featured the game's first live play-by-play announcer, 26-year-old Harold Arlin.[8]

54. The first-ever television broadcast of a major league baseball game was on August 26, 1939, when the Cincinnati Reds played a doubleheader against the Brooklyn Dodgers at Ebbets Field.[8]

55. Sandy Koufax is the youngest player ever elected to the Baseball Hall of Fame and, when one overall Cy Young award was given

LIL DIAMONDS

for all of Major League Baseball instead of one award for each league, he won three times by unanimous vote.

56. The oldest player to hit a home run was Julio Franco (1958–) of the New York Mets. He was 47 years and 240 days old when he hit a home run on April 20, 2006.[8]

57. Greg Maddox (Atlanta Braves) was the first pitcher in Major League Baseball history to win the Cy Young Award four consecutive years (1992-1995).

58. A baseball pitcher's curveball can curve over 17 inches away from a straight line toward home plate.[6]

59. In 1931, Chattanooga shortstop Johnny Jones was traded to the Charlotte Hornets for a 25-pound turkey. Equally bizarre was when Jack Fenton was traded to San Francisco of the Pacific Coast League for a bag of prunes. The most famous sale in baseball history took place in 1919 when the Yankees paid Boston $125,000 for Babe Ruth.[4]

60. In 1930, Babe Ruth was making $80,000, which is about $1 million in current money. When he was asked how he deserved to make more than the U.S. president, he replied, "I had a better year."[8]

61. Many people believe that Abner Doubleday (1819–1893) invented baseball in 1839 in Cooperstown, New York. However, baseball actually slowly evolved from simple European bat-and-ball games that were played in the 18th and 19th centuries.[8]

62. Some of the most famous baseball records include Joe DiMaggio's 56-game hitting streak, Ted William's .407 batting average in 1941, Barry Bonds' 73 homers in 2001, and Cy Young's 511 career wins.[8]

63. Baseball has been called America's national pastime since the Civil War. Indeed, its popularity increased during that war (1861–65) as both Union and Confederate soldiers played the game as a morale booster and emotional escape when they had time.[8]

64. George Herman Ruth, Jr. (Babe Ruth) was nicknamed "Babe" when a player saw Baltimore Orioles manager Jack Dunn with

his new player and said, "There goes Dunnie with his new babe."[8]

65. Babe Ruth (also nicknamed "Bambino," "The Big Bam," and "The Sultan of Swap") hit his first home run on May 6, 1915, off New York Yankees pitcher Jack Warhop. Ruth helped revolutionize baseball by transforming it into a power-hitting game.[4]

66. Harry Wright (1835–1895), a former cricket player and businessman, organized the first professional baseball team, the Cincinnati Red Stockings, in 1869. He signed nine players to contracts at an average annual salary of $950. The Red Stockings played their first game on March 15, 1869, against Antioch College, winning 41-7.[8]

67. In the same year the NNL was created, the Negro Southern League was formed by Thomas T. Wilson by bringing together the all Black teams located below the Mason-Dixon. Teams from Nashville, Atlanta, Birmingham, Memphis, Montgomery and New Orleans united to play the game in a "safe environment" within the segregated south.

68. The first professional baseball league was the National Association of Professional Baseball Players. It was formed during the winter of 1870, when Harry Wright of the Cincinnati Red Stockings broke away from the National Association of Baseball Players, which still claimed to be for amateurs only.[8]

69. In baseball history, "The Dead Ball Era" refers to the years 1900–1919 when baseballs were soft and loosely wound, which made them harder to hit far. Consequently, the pitchers of the day, such as Cy Young, Walter Johnson, and Grover Cleveland had a clear advantage over hitters (though there were also prolific hitters of that time, such as Ty Cobb, Joe Jackson, and Honus Wagner).[8]

70. In 1885, the Cuban Giants formed the first black professional baseball team.

71. In addition to "pitcher's elbow" and rotator cuff injuries, the worst shoulder injury for a baseball pitcher is a labrum tear, or when the cartilage between the upper arm and the shoulder

socket tears. A torn labrum usually requires surgery, and very few pitchers have a successful career afterward.[6]

72. It is a rule that a pitcher must first wipe his hand on his uniform before he grips the ball for a pitch.[4]

73. The catcher has one of the most difficult jobs in baseball. Even with the extra padding in a glove, catchers often develop circulatory problems in their hand from catching so many powerful pitches. Catchers often also suffer from torn meniscus.[6]

74. A baseball catcher's equipment is sometimes called "tools of ignorance" because it is said that catching is such a difficult job that no intelligent person would do it.[4]

75. Tony Clark is the first African American and first former player to be appointed Executive Director of the MLB Player's Union.

76. Evar Swanson (1902–1973), a left fielder for baseball's Cincinnati Reds, holds the record for the fastest time around the bases. On September 15, 1929, he ran the bases in 13.3 seconds, a record that has held for over 80 years.[8]

77. The fastest baseball ever thrown anywhere is usually credited to Cleveland Indian pitcher Bob Feller. In 1946, he threw a fastball at 107.9 mph during a pitching display at Griffith Field. The Guinness Book of World Records sites a 2010 pitch by Aroldis Chapman as the fastest, at 105.1 mph during a Reds' game against the San Diego Pedros.[7]

78. Glen Gorbous (1930–1990) holds the record for the longest throw by a pro baseball player. During a throwing exhibition in 1957, with a running start, he threw the ball 445 feet, 10 inches (136 meters).[8]

79. In 1882, players wore colored jerseys according to the position they played, not the team they played for. In 1883, owners ruled each team could choose its own uniform, except the stockings, which would be decided by the leagues.[4]

80. "Cranks" was an early term for baseball fans in the late 1880s. The term "fan" is said to be a shortened form of "fanatic."[4]

81. The term "Murderer's Row" describes the 1927 Yankee lineup, which featured future Baseball Hall of Famers Babe Ruth, Lou Gehrig, Bob Meusel, Tony Lazzeri, and Earle Combs.[4]

82. Alexander Cartwright (1820–1892) organized the first ever baseball team named the Knickerbocker Baseball Club of New York, named after a New York City fire department. He also helped create the first-ever written rules of baseball in 1845 and was the first to draft the baseball diamond. He is one of several people named the "Father of Baseball."[8]

83. Known (among several others) as the "Father of Baseball," sportswriter Henry Chadwick of the New York Clipper increased baseball's popularity by reporting games and inventing an early version of the box score. He is also the only writer to have been elected into the Baseball Hall of Fame.[6]

84. A major league baseball must have lacing with exactly 108 stitches. It also must have a circumference between 9.00 and 9.25 inches, a weight between 5.00 and 5.25 ounces, and two pieces of cowhide laced together with red-waxed cotton stitches.[6]

85. All baseball fields have certain features in common. The distance between the bases is always exactly 90 feet (27 meters). The pitching rubber, where the pitcher stands, is 60 feet 6 inches (18 meters) from the back tip of home plate.[6]

86. An average of 50 foul balls are hit during a major league baseball game

87. During the average major league baseball game, 50 foul balls are hit into a crowd of about 31,000 people.[8]

88. The youngest pitcher in major league baseball history is Joe Nuxhall (1928–2007) who was just 15 years old when he entered a game and pitched 2/3 of an inning for the Cincinatti Reds.[8]

89. Cal Ripken Jr. holds the record for playing in the most consecutive baseball games. He played in 2,632 games and was twice named the American League's Most Valuable Player, in 1983 and 1991. He didn't miss a game in 16 years.[8]

90. Pete Rose (1941–) from the Cincinnati Reds holds the all-time record for hits (4,256) and games played (3,562). He was banned from baseball for life for betting on games while managing the team.[8]
91. The National Baseball Hall of Fame is located in Cooperstown, New York, and was established in 1935. The first five men elected to "Cooperstown," as it is also known, were Ty Cobb, Babe Ruth, Honus Wagner, Christy Mathewson, and Walter Johnson.[8]
92. Philadelphia Phillies star Richie Ashburn (1927–1997) fouled off two consecutive pitches that hit the same woman twice in the stands. The first foul ball broke the woman's nose. While medics were attending to her, Ashburn hit a second foul ball that hit the same woman as she was being carried off on a stretcher.[8]
93. The Atlanta Braves team, which originated in Boston, at one time were called the Beaneaters after the area's famous Boston Baked Beans. In 1912, the name was changed to the Braves.[8]
94. While Jackie Robinson is commonly thought to be the first African-American baseball player in the big leagues when he played on April 15, 1947, another African-American named William Edward White played a single game for the National League's Providence Grays on June 21, 1879, making him the first.[8]
95. Baseball was a full medal sport in the Olympics from 1992–2008. However, a vote by the International Olympic Committee took baseball off the calendar starting in 2012. World baseball groups continue to try to return the sport to the games.[5]
96. In 1943, with the major leagues depleted due to WW II, Chicago Cubs owner Philip Wrigley started a professional women's softball team to attract fan interest. The team eventually switched from playing softball (pitching underhand) to baseball and changed their name to the All-American Girls Baseball League (AAGBL). The AAGBL played their final season in 1954.[8]

97. To achieve the crosshatched diamond pattern on a baseball field, rollers on a mower push the grass slightly forward, similar to running a vacuum back and forth on a plush carpet. Blades bent away from the viewer capture more light and appear paler. Grass blades that are bent toward the viewer look darker.[1]

98. In his Baseball Hall of Fame induction speech in 1966, Ted Williams made a strong plea for inclusion of Negro league stars in the Hall.

99. The members of the Hall who played in both the Negro leagues and Major League Baseball are Hank Aaron, Ernie Banks, Roy Campanella, Larry Doby, Willie Mays, and Jackie Robinson. Except for Doby, their play in the Negro leagues was a minor factor in their selection: Aaron, Banks, and Mays played in Negro leagues only briefly and after the leagues had declined with the migration of many black players to the integrated minor leagues.

100. Hank Aaron was the last Negro league player to hold a regular position in Major League Baseball.

REFERENCES

1 Branch, John. "Groundskeepers Display Artistry on the Diamond." New York Times. September 30, 2008. Accessed: October 20, 2015.

2. Encyclopedia Brittanica 2Brown, Maury. "Major League Baseball Sees Record $9 Billion in Revenues for 2014." Forbes. December 10, 2014. Accessed: October 19, 2015.

3 Buckley, James. Baseball (DK Eyewitness Books). New York, NY: DK Publishing, 2010.

4 Cook, Sally and James Charlton. Hey Batta Batta Swing!: The Wild Old Days of Baseball. New York, NY: Margaret K. McElderry Books, 2007.

5 Denomme, Ian. "Will Baseball Return to the Olympics? We'll Know in 2016." Yahoo. February 5, 2015. Accessed: November 7, 2015.

6 Dreier, David. Baseball: How It Works (Sports Illustrated for Kids). Mankato, MN: Capstone Press, 2010.

7 "Fastest Baseball Pitch (Male)." Guinness World Records. 2015. Accessed: October 13, 2015.

8 Fischer, David. Baseball (Smithsonian Q & A: The Ultimate Question and Answer Book). Irvington, NY: Hyrda Publishing, 2007.

9 "Hot Dogs Remain Top Dog for Major League Baseball Fans." GlobeNewswire. March 28, 2014. Accessed: October 19, 2015.

10 Levkoff, Logan. Third Base Ain't What It Used to Be. New York, NY: Open Road Media, 2012.

11 Palmer, Alex. Weird-o-pedia. New York, NY: Skyhorse Publishing, 2012.

12 Smith, Kyle. "The 10 Best Baseball Movies of All Time." New York Post. May 14, 2014. Accessed: October 20, 2015.

13 Stewart, Sara. "Will a Woman Ever Play in the Major Leagues?" New York Post. August 23, 2014. Accessed: October 19, 2015.

14 "The History of Ballpark Food." History.com. March 31, 2011. Accessed: October 19, 2015.

LIL DIAMONDS

Under the guidance of his father, Reggie began playing sports at five years old. Through practice, commitment, and focus, he excelled in high school, where he played three years on the varsity baseball team. He was named to the New York Daily News All-State Team two years in a row.

Reggie was recruited by dozens of colleges and chose Northwestern University, a member of the Big Ten Conference. As he was completing his Junior year, he was drafted by the Seattle Mariners but turned down the offer to continue his studies. Following graduation, Reggie was drafted by the Pittsburgh Pirates and played in their minor league organization for four years. During his career, he played against three MLB Hall of Famers – Greg Maddox, Barry Larkin and Roberto Alomar and with or against stars such as Barry Bonds, Bobby Bonilla, Rafael Palmeiro, Ellis Burks, and Joe Girardi. A wrist injury ended his professional playing career, but he never lost his love of the sport.

Once his career ended, Reggie used his energy, determination, and drive to become a certified New Jersey high school History teacher and then went on to Wall Street to become a licensed wealth manager.

Reggie lives by a simple creed: (1) God first; (2) work hard; and (3) be the best you can be...always. He hopes that this book will inspire the next generation of baseball players and those that support them.

LIL **DIAMONDS**
BASEBALL GEMS IN THE MAKING!

www.lildiamondsbaseball.com

Made in the USA
Columbia, SC
22 January 2021